Ocean Adventures

The Indian Ocean

Written by
Rebecca Phillips-Bartlett

KidHaven Publishing

Published in 2026 by
KidHaven Publishing, an Imprint of Greenhaven Publishing, LLC
2544 Clinton St., Buffalo, NY 14224

Written by: Rebecca Phillips-Bartlett
Edited by: Noah Leatherland
Designed by: Ker Ker Lee

Cataloging-in-Publication Data
Names: Phillips-Bartlett, Rebecca, 1999-.
Title: The Indian Ocean / Rebecca Phillips-Bartlett.
Description: Buffalo, NY : KidHaven Publishing, 2026. | Series: Ocean adventures | Includes glossary and index.
Identifiers: ISBN 9781534552036 (pbk.) | ISBN 9781534552043 (library bound) | ISBN 9781534552050 (ebook)
Subjects: LCSH: Indian Ocean--Juvenile literature. | Marine ecology--Indian Ocean--Juvenile literature.
Classification: LCC GC721.P45 2026 | DDC 551.46'15--dc23

Printed in China

CPSIA compliance information: Batch #QW26KH: For further information contact Greenhaven Publishing LLC at 1-844-317-7404.

Please visit our website, www.greenhavenpublishing.com. For a free color catalog of all our high-quality books, call toll free 1-844-317-7404 or fax 1-844-317-7405.

Find us on

Photo Credits – Images courtesy of Shutterstock.com, unless otherwise stated.

Cover & Recurring – karacacennet, Nastya Vaulina, alazur. 2–3 – Pandora Pictures. 4–5 – Kingppin, Poznyakov. 6–7 – ESB Professional, Viacheslav Lopatin. 8–9 – GUDKOV ANDREY, Miroslav Halama. 10–11 – Aylata, Harmonise Creatives. 12–13 – mc_pongsatorn, David Keep, Rich Carey. 14–15 – vkilikov, Katiekk. 16–17 – EarnestTse, Don Mammoser. 18–19 – Tomas Kotouc, Henryp982. 20–21 – kaetana, Guido Vermeulen-Perdaen. 22–23 – Jag_cz, RomanMr.

CONTENTS

WORDS THAT LOOK LIKE THIS CAN BE FOUND IN THE GLOSSARY ON PAGE 24.

OCEAN ADVENTURES

Ahoy there, sailor! Are you ready to explore the ocean? Then climb aboard! It is time to go on an ocean adventure. Oceans are large pools of salt water. Most of Earth is covered by five main oceans.

Oceans are home to many amazing plants, animals, and other living things. These living things are all connected. This connected group is called an ecosystem.

THE INDIAN OCEAN

The Indian Ocean is the warmest ocean on Earth. Some animals need this warmth to stay healthy. Lots of animals in the Indian Ocean cannot be found anywhere else on the planet.

THE INDIAN OCEAN WAS EXPLORED BEFORE THE PACIFIC AND ATLANTIC OCEANS.

The Indian Ocean is between Africa, Asia, Australia, and Antarctica. This ocean is a very important trade route. Ships carry items over the Indian Ocean to be sold in other countries.

PLACES OF INTEREST IN THE INDIAN OCEAN

The Migration Corridor

It is not only ships that travel through the Indian Ocean. Many animals migrate through the Indian Ocean. Humpback whales migrate through a path called the migration corridor.

MANY HUMPBACK WHALES HAVE YOUNG IN THE INDIAN OCEAN. THEY MIGRATE TO COLDER WATERS TO FIND FOOD.

Incredible Islands

An island is a bit of land that is surrounded by water. The Indian Ocean is home to more than 1,000 islands, including Madagascar and Christmas Island.

Madagascar is the largest island in the Indian Ocean. It has many smaller islands around it.

WEATHER

The Indian Ocean has a big impact on the weather in parts of Africa and Asia. Strong winds called monsoons blow over the Indian Ocean. They carry lots of rain toward Africa and Asia.

Monsoon rainfall can last many months. Places that get monsoons have a wet season and a dry season. Many farmers in Africa and Asia rely on monsoon rains to grow their crops.

FISH

Clownfish

The warm Indian Ocean is perfect for clownfish. These colorful fish live in creatures called anemones. Anemones have powerful stinging tentacles. Clownfish are covered in goo that protects them from the sting.

Manta Rays

Manta rays are large fish. They do not travel alone. Fish called remoras often catch a ride on rays. Remoras eat bits of the rays' skin. This keeps the rays healthy and feeds the remoras.

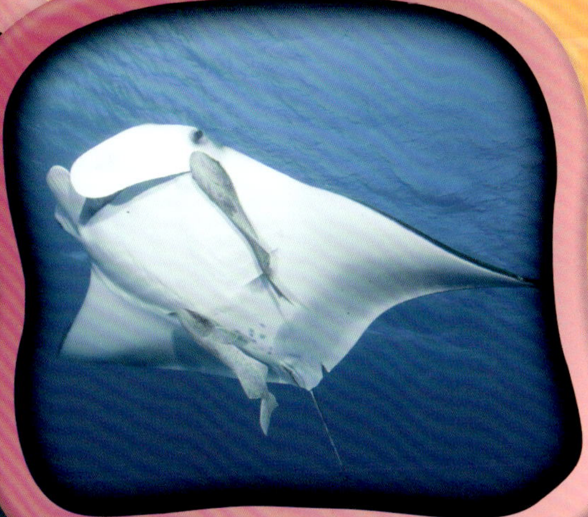

MAMMALS

Dugongs

Dugongs mostly live in seagrass meadows in warm oceans. Dugongs are herbivores, which means they only eat plants. Seagrass meadows give them a place to shelter and food to eat.

Humpback Dolphins

Indian Ocean humpback dolphins mostly live in shallow waters near land. These mammals live in groups called pods. Just like people talk to each other, dolphins whistle to communicate with other dolphins in their pod.

BIRDS

Black-Naped Terns

Black-naped terns have white feathers with a black band over their eyes. They fly over warm oceans hunting for food. When they spot a fish, they dip their beaks into the water to grab it.

Great Frigatebirds

Great frigatebirds fly over warm oceans, including the Indian Ocean and parts of the Pacific and Atlantic Oceans. They are most well-known for their bright red neck pouches.

MALE FRIGATEBIRDS USE THEIR NECK POUCHES TO ATTRACT A MATE.

OTHER ANIMALS

Sea Snakes

Many different types of sea snakes live in the Indian Ocean. Sea snakes breathe air but spend most of their time underwater. Some kinds of sea snakes can "breathe" through their skin!

SOME SEA SNAKES ARE VERY <u>VENOMOUS</u>!

Box Jellyfish

Box jellyfish are some of the most venomous sea creatures in the world. They can grow up to 15 stinging tentacles. Unlike most jellyfish, which drift through the water, box jellyfish are powerful swimmers.

OUR CHANGING OCEANS

Our oceans exist in a balance. If one thing changes, it can cause harmful changes for other parts of the ocean. The Indian Ocean is changing because of human actions.

Many ships that cross the Indian Ocean are spilling oil or dropping trash.

Lots of waste from factories gets dropped into the ocean. This harms the living things that need the water to survive. We can all help protect the oceans by thinking carefully about what we buy.

EXPLORING THE OCEAN

There is so much to explore in the Indian Ocean. As we explore, it is important to think about the living things that call the ocean home. We must protect and respect their ocean home.

Some ocean animals can be dangerous. Watch out for venomous jellyfish and slippery sea snakes! Which ocean animal would you most like to meet on your adventure?

GLOSSARY

crops plants that are grown to be used by humans, such as to make food or clothes

mammals animals that are warm-blooded, have a backbone, and make milk to feed their young

mate a partner of the same species that an animal has young with

migrate when animals move from one place to another based on changes in weather, for food, or to have young

venomous able to inject a harmful substance called venom through a bite or a sting

INDEX